3 1160 00480 3081

D1609120

BLOOMFIELD TOWNSHIP PUBLIC LIBRARY
1099 Lone Pine Road
Bloomfield Hills, Michigan 48302-2410

Mount
Fitz Roy
Viewed From
Los Glaciares
National Park

FACES AND PLACES

ARGENTINA

BLOOMFIELD TOWNSHIP PUBLIC LIBRARY
1099 Lone Pine Road
Bloomfield Hills, Michigan 48302-2410

BY KATHRYN STEVENS

THE CHILD'S WORLD®, INC.

GRAPHIC DESIGN AND PRODUCTION
Robert E. Bonaker / Graphic Design & Consulting Co.

PHOTO RESEARCH
James R. Rothaus / James R. Rothaus & Associates

COVER PHOTO
Portrait of an Argentinian boy at a Patagonia ranch
©Caroline Penn/CORBIS

Text copyright © 2001 by The Child's World®, Inc.
All rights reserved. No part of this book may be reproduced
or utilized in any form or by any means without written
permission from the publisher.
Printed in the United States of America.

Library of Congress Cataloging-in-Publication Data
Stevens, Kathryn, 1954-
Argentina / by Kathryn Stevens.
p. cm.
Includes index.
Summary: Describes the history, geography, people, and
customs of the South American country, Argentina.
ISBN 1-56766-712-0 (lib. bdg. : alk. paper)

1. Argentina — Juvenile literature.
[1. Argentina.] I. Title.

F2808.2 .S74 2000   99-042407
982 21 — dc21

Table
of
Contents

AUG 9 2001

If you could fly high above Earth, you would see enormous land areas called **continents**. The continents are mostly surrounded by water. Argentina lies near the pointed southern tip of a continent called South America.

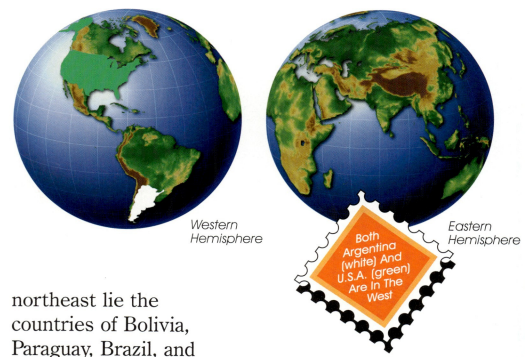

Western Hemisphere

Eastern Hemisphere

Both Argentina (white) And U.S.A. (green) Are In The West

Along the east side of Argentina is the Atlantic Ocean. To the north and northeast lie the countries of Bolivia, Paraguay, Brazil, and Uruguay. To the west lies the long, narrow nation of Chile.

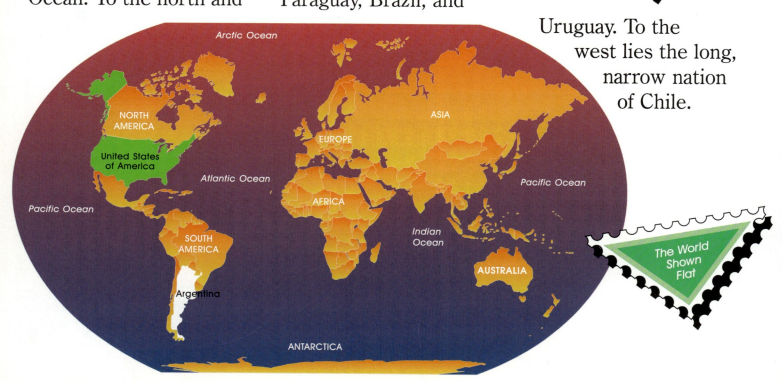

Arctic Ocean

NORTH AMERICA

United States of America

Atlantic Ocean

Pacific Ocean

EUROPE

ASIA

AFRICA

Pacific Ocean

Indian Ocean

SOUTH AMERICA

Argentina

AUSTRALIA

ANTARCTICA

The World Shown Flat

BOLIVIA

BRAZIL

CHILE

PARAGUAY

Pacific
Ocean

URUGUAY

ARGENTINA

Atlantic
Ocean

FALKLAND ISLANDS

Close-Up
of
Argentina

Iguazú Falls
Is On The
Border
Between
Argentina
And Brazil

Iguazú Falls

ANDES MOUNTAINS

Mount
Aconagua

PAMPA

★ Buenos Aires

Mount Fitz Roy

PATAGONIA

TIERRA DEL FUEGO

Argentina's land ranges from arid deserts to snowy mountains. In the north are broad lowlands, some of them moist and tropical. Eastern and central Argentina have low, flat plains called the *pampa* (PAHM-pah). The pampa's rich soils are ideal for growing crops. Farther south are the flat, raised **plateaus** of Patagonia. Patagonia's plateaus are dry, windswept, and cool.

Coast Of Tierra del Fuego

CORBIS/Wolfgang Kaehler

Cuernos del Paine Mountains In Patagonia

The high, rugged Andes Mountains run all along the western side of Argentina. The highest mountain in North and South America lies in Argentina's Andes. This mountain, called *Aconcagua*, is almost 23,000 feet tall!

Plants & Animals

Because the land varies so much, Argentina has a wide variety of plants. Forests grow in some parts of the Andes and a few other regions. Cool, dry Patagonia is covered with grasses and low shrubs. Grasses also cover much of the pampa. Much of Argentina's land is too dry for growing crops. These dry areas are farmed by **irrigation**, or bringing in river water.

Argentina has many different kinds of animals. The Andes are home to shaggy, camel-like llamas and vicuña. In other regions, monkeys, deer, foxes, and wild cats called *jaguars* and *pumas* still roam. Argentina has had lots of animals for millions of years. Some of the world's most interesting fossils are found in Argentina—including dinosaurs and giant penguins.

CORBIS/Enzo & Paolo Ragazzini

A Giant Cactus In The Desert Region Of Patagonia

A Rhea Standing In The Grass Near Goya

CORBIS/Peter Johnson

CORBIS/Galen Rowell

•Goya

PATAGONIA   VALDEZ PENINSULA

Magellanic Penguins On The Valdes Peninsula

The Ruins Of A Building On A Cliff At Puerte de Inca

Puerte de Inca

★Buenos Aires

CORBIS/Hubert Stadler

Thousands of years ago, Argentina, like the rest of South America, was populated by Native Americans. In the 1500s, Spanish and Portuguese explorers and soldiers came to the region. They conquered the native peoples and claimed the area as a **colony** ruled by Spain.

In the early 1800s, Argentina began to fight for independence. Many years of civil war followed. People had different ideas about how the country should be run. Some wanted a strong government based at Buenos Aires. Others wanted more local independence. Unrest continued through much of the 1800s.

CORBIS/Gianni Dagli Orti

Portuguese Explorer Ferdinand Magellan, Who Landed In Argentina In 1519

British Troops Attacking Buenos Aires In 1807

CORBIS/Bettmann

Argentina Today

Between 1930 and 1983, Argentina was ruled by strong governments that gave the people little freedom. The most famous ruler was Juan Perón, president from 1946 to 1955. Perón improved some conditions for workers but ruled with an iron hand. Military leaders in the late 1970s ruled even more harshly, killing thousands of people who opposed them.

Former President Juan Perón Seated At His Desk In Buenos Aires

CORBIS/Bettmann

Plaza Mayo In Buenos Aires During The Revolution Of 1943

CORBIS/Bettmann

Today, Argentina is governed by a president and a congress. The president still has a great deal of power, but not as much as in earlier times. Now the congress plays a much stronger role. People between the ages of 19 and 70 are required to vote in elections.

Buenos Aires

CORBIS/Pablo Corral Vega

The
Argentinian
Congress
Building In
Buenos Aires

CORBIS/Macduff Everton

A Singer
Performing
On The
Street In
San Telmo

Pampas

Buenos Aires
San Telmo

Gauchos At A Rodeo In Pampas

CORBIS/Barnabas Bosshart

Many of Argentina's people were **immigrants** who came from other lands. Most of the earlier immigrants came from Italy, Spain, and other European countries. A smaller number were brought from Africa as slaves. Today, most Argentines come from families with European backgrounds. Others come from families with mixed European and Native American backgrounds.

A Guard Outside The Presidential Mansion In Buenos Aires

CORBIS/Dave G. Houser

Nine out of ten people in Argentina belong to the Roman Catholic faith. A much smaller number follow Protestant, Jewish, or other faiths. Argentines place a great deal of importance on family life and loyalty to family and friends.

A House In The Hills Of Patagonia

CORBIS/Caroline Penn

Most of Argentina's people live in cities. In fact, over one-third live in the capital city of Buenos Aires and its nearby **suburbs**. Buenos Aires is a fast-paced city where people are busy day and night. Many people have moved from Argentina's countryside to the cities to look for work. Overcrowding has become a problem, especially in Buenos Aires.

Fewer than one in three Argentines live in the country. Many work on farms or large ranches called *estancias* (eh-STAHN-see-ahs), or "estates." Hired hands who herd cattle are called *gauchos* (GOW-chohz). Like North American cowboys, gauchos once roamed the country on horseback, chasing free-running cattle. Their rough, colorful way of life changed as the ranch lands were fenced—but their tradition continues.

Ushuaia Is One Of The World's Southernmost Cities

CORBIS/Galen Rowell

CORBIS/Pablo Corral Vega

★ Buenos Aires

PATAGONIA

Ushuaia

The Capital
City Of
Buenos Aires
At Night

Signs
Crowd Main
Street In
Salta

•Salta

★Buenos Aires

CORBIS/Enzo & Paolo Ragazzini

Schools And Language

Schoolgirls In Uniform Crossing A Street In Buenos Aires

Between the ages of 6 and 14, all Argentine children must attend primary school. There they learn a variety of subjects, including math, reading, and writing. Many students decide to go on to secondary schools, though not all of them graduate. Some students also go on to universities.

The most widely spoken language is Argentine Spanish, or *Castellano*. It is a bit different from the Spanish language spoken in Spain. It even includes words from Italian, brought by Italian immigrants. Different regions have their own versions, or **dialects**, of Argentine Spanish.

CORBIS/Pablo Corral Vega

Argentina's Native Americans spoke many different languages, some of which are also still in use.

CORBIS/Michael S. Yamashita

Students In A Computer Class In Buenos Aires

Argentina's people work in a wide range of jobs. Many work in shops, banks, or offices. About 20 percent work in manufacturing plants that process food or make steel, machinery, chemicals, or other products. Some work in the oil industry, processing gasoline and other oil-based products.

An Engineer Works On An Old Steam Train Between El Maiten And Esquel

CORBIS/Hubert Stadler

Some people work on the nation's farms and ranches. About one-tenth of Argentina's land is used for growing crops such as wheat, corn and many kinds of fruit. Many of these crops are sold to other countries. About 40 percent of the land is used for raising livestock, especially cattle and sheep. Ranchers raise livestock to sell the meat, wool, and other products.

Gauchos Tie A Cow On A Ranch In Patagonia

CORBIS/Hubert Stadler

CORBIS/Robert van der Hilst

Buenos Aires

Esquel • El Maiten

PATAGONIA

TIERRA DEL FUEGO

A Young
Sheepshearer
On A Sheep Ranch
In Tierra del
Fuego

Enjoying
A Meal On
A Patio
In Palermo

Buenos Aires ★ Palermo

CORBIS/Pablo Corral Vega

A Produce Stand At A Buenos Aires Market

CORBIS/Owen Franken

Argentines enjoy many tasty foods. Different regions have their own local specialties. Meats, especially beef, are a big part of the diet. Some people eat beef at every meal. Meats are roasted, grilled, stewed, or made into sausages. Roasting meat over an open fire is especially popular. *Empanadas* are small pies stuffed with spiced meat and other fillings.

Empanadas On A Sailboat In Buenos Aires

CORBIS/Owen Franken

An everyday drink is *yerba maté* (ZHAIR-ba mah-TEH), a tea made from the leaves of a native holly tree. Argentina also makes a large amount of wine and sells it all over the world. Grapes are grown and made into wine at **vineyards**.

Pastimes And Holidays

Argentines enjoy reading, fine art, and going to theaters and movies. In towns, people sit at outdoor cafés drinking coffee, visiting, or playing chess. Music of all kinds is popular, from rock to opera. Dancing is popular, too—including the graceful, stylish dance called the *tango*. Different regions have their own types of music and dance.

Argentines love sports, too. Soccer, also called football (*fútbol*), is especially popular. Many people also enjoy tennis, rugby, horse racing, polo, basketball, golf, boating, boxing, and auto racing. In the mountains, people like to ski. Along the coast, they sunbathe and swim in the ocean.

Argentines celebrate a variety of holidays. They hold parades on New Year's Day (January 1) and Labor Day (May 1) and exchange gifts at Christmas (December 25). The Anniversary of the Revolution (May 25) celebrates the day in 1810 when Argentina began to form its own government.

Independence Day is July 9. Different regions also celebrate their own *fiestas* (festivals) with music, dancing, and feasts.

Argentina is a scenic and exciting country. If you visit Argentina, you can go swimming in the ocean or skiing in the mountains. You can roam the busy streets of Buenos Aires, or watch gauchos herding cattle on an *estancia*. There are plenty of things to see and do in Argentina!

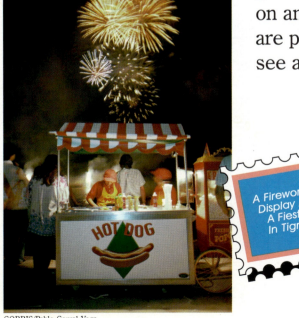

CORBIS/Pablo Corral Vega

A Fireworks Display At A Fiesta In Tigre

Buenos Aires★ •Tigre

+ Cerros dos Picos

FALKLAND ISLANDS

CORBIS/Nik Wheeler

Argentina Playing in The World Cup Soccer Match In Buenos Aires In 1978

Area
Almost 1.1 million square miles (2.8 million square kilometers)—about one-third the size of the United States.

Population
About 35 million people.

Capital City
Buenos Aires (BWAY-nos AR-ez).

Other Important Cities
Córdoba, Rosario, La Plata, and Mendoza.

Important Rivers
The Paraná, Paraguay, Uruguay, Colorado, Negro (NEH-groh), and Chubut.

Money
The nuevo peso argentino (NWAY-voh PEH-soh ahr-jen-TEEN-oh, or "new Argentine peso").

National Flag
A flag with two light blue stripes and one white stripe. When Argentines protested for independence in the early 1800s, blue and white were the protesters' colors. The sun in the white stripe stands for the sun that shone on the protesters.

National Song
"Himno Nacional Argentino," or "Argentine National Anthem."

Official Name
The Argentine Republic.

Head of Government
The president of Argentina.

Horseback
Riding Near
The Cerros
dos Picos
Mountains In
Patagonia

Did You Know?

Argentina is the second-largest nation in South America. Only Brazil is bigger. Argentina is also the eighth-largest nation in the world.

"Argentina" means "silvery" in Spanish. When Spanish explorers saw the Native Americans' silver ornaments, they thought Argentina's silver would make them rich. They were unhappy with how little silver they found.

The musical play and movie Evita! are about Eva Perón, the popular wife of former president Juan Perón. "Evita" was Eva Perón's nickname.

In 1982, Argentina fought a war with Great Britain over the Falkland Islands, a small group of islands off the Argentine coast. Argentina lost the war, and the Falklands remained under British control.

Iguazú Falls is a gigantic waterfall along Argentina's border with Brazil. It is bigger than North America's Niagara Falls. People come from all over the world to see this beautiful sight.

How Do You Say?

	ARGENTINE SPANISH	HOW TO SAY IT
Good Morning	buenos días	BWEH–nos DEE–ahs
	buongiorno	bohn–ZHYOR–noh
Good-bye	adiós	ah–dee–OSE
	chau	CHOW
Please	por favor	por fah–VOR
Thank You	gracias	GRAH–see–ahs
One	uno	OO–noh
Two	dos	DOSE
Three	tres	TRACE
Yes	sí	SEE
No	no	NO

colony (KOL–uh–nee)
A colony is a land ruled by a faraway country. Argentina was once a colony ruled by distant Spain.

continents (KON–tih–nents)
Continents are enormous areas of land mostly surrounded by water. Argentina lies at the southern tip of the continent of South America.

dialects (DY–uh–lekts)
Dialects are different versions of a language. Argentina has a number of different dialects of Spanish.

immigrants (IH–mih–grents)
Immigrants are newcomers who move to a country from somewhere else. Many immigrants moved to Argentina from Europe.

irrigation (eer–ih–GAY–shun)
Irrigation is pumping river water onto dry fields so crops can grow. Much of Argentina's farmland must be irrigated.

plateaus (pla–TOHS)
Plateaus are raised "tables" of land that are higher than the land around them. Argentina's Patagonia is a region of plateaus.

suburbs (SUB–urbs)
Suburbs are smaller communities around the outside of a city. Many people live in the suburbs of Argentina's capital, Buenos Aires.

vineyards (VIN–yerdz)
Vineyards are places where grapes are grown and made into wine. Argentina's vineyards produce fine wines sold around the world.

Index

Web Sites

Learn more about Argentina:
http://www.lonelyplanet.com/dest/sam/argie.htm
http://www.interknowledge.com/argentina

Learn more about Evita Perón:
http://www.evitaperon.org/

Learn how to make some Argentinian foods:
http://soar.berkeley.edu/recipes/ethnic/argentina/